Joe Bob Briggs
Host of TNT's MONSTERVISION
Drive-In Movie Critic &
All Around Bimbo Historian

Let's Talk

Strictly speaking, I've watched 68,000 B movies. I have actually offered my brain to the U.S. Department of Justice, encouraging them to conduct studies to determine whether an unhealthy diet of excruciating horror can lead to violent or sexually deviant behavior. All of my ex-wives are prepared to testify in the affirmative. But in another sense I've only watched one movie, a movie that happens to be 136,000 hours long. Any producer, writer, actor or critic in the horror field knows exactly what I'm talking about. There are rules for this sort of thing, and they don't change much from picture to picture. There are standards. They were first set out by Aristotle, in the chapter of his "Poetics" dealing with "ars terrora," in which he said: "The zombies must rise. The dead must walk. The girl in the Frederick's of Hollywood baby-doll chemise must recoil ' in extremis.'" But the greeks had a pessimistic view of human nature. When they watched "Medea," they EXPECTED to see that crazy bitch butcher them babies. Americans,to this day, can watch the "Psycho" shower scene and a tiny rear brain lobe will be wispering, "Maybe she'll make it." Hence this valuable guide to the American public's willingness to believe that the fat girl on the side of the road won't get skewered by Jason, the class slut will survive the prom, and the boyfriend of Kimberly the beach bunny will turn out to be a nice guy after all. My friend Debbie Rochon knows that there's a price to be paid for being beautiful in a B movie, and it usually comes in the form of red Karo syrup poured in a gaping Latex head wound. Can these situations be avoided ? Probably not. But "The B Movie Survival Guide" is the closest you'll ever come to a primer for the optimistic victim who just won't say die.

The B-Movie Survival Guide
Horror • Sci-Fi • Action • Erotic Thrillers

Written By:
Gary Cook
Debbie Rochon
Peter Schmideg

Illustrations By:
Dave Gatzmer

Published by Wild Things, a division of Image Group 529 S. 7th St. #219 Minneapolis,MN.55415
ISBN 0-9669817-0-7 printed in the USA

BASIC TRAINING

Never

go skinny-dipping.

If you must

take that cursed

midnight swim

wear as much

clothing as possible.

Think Layers

It will help later

when you're

SCREAMING

running away

through the woods from a

disembodied spirit,

and all those

dreaded branches

are scraping against

your limbs.

Don't
buy toys that
TALK or WALK

While teenagers
are smarter
than their parents,
little kids are
even smarter
than teenagers

If you're a kid,
it's **OK;**
only adults and
teenagers
get mutilated

Don't

Take Anything

From

The Dead !

Never

Pick Up

A Stranger

If He or She

Is Wearing A

Santa Claus Suit.

If you have just
killed the monster
(yeah right)
this is not the time
to hug, kiss, grope
your significant other......
RUN !

Even if

you really think

you have killed

the monster...
KILL
IT
AGAIN !

Remember
when going to a party
at an old abandoned house...
Comfortable Shoes, it's hard
to run through the woods
in heels.

If
you are running through the woods
being chased by a killer,
you will fall down a couple of times.
Allow yourself extra time.

By all means,
bargain with Satan;
but please don't sell your soul.
Negotiate !
If money is truly
the root of all evil,
then SATAN
appeciates
free enterprise.

If
the guy
terrorizing you
on the phone
during a storm
already knows
your name

OR

what
you're wearing...
GIVE UP .

If
you have
killed the maniac,
don't
try to uncover
his face
to see who he is.
CUT
the head off first,
then check.

This may sound selfish
but;
everyone else is expendable.
This is the
Me Me Me
principle.

Even Though
You Can BuyA Ouija Board
At A Toy Store,
Remember:
Anything That You Can
Throw Away Or Burn That
Still Comes Back And Is Used
To Speak To The Dead
IS NOT A TOY !

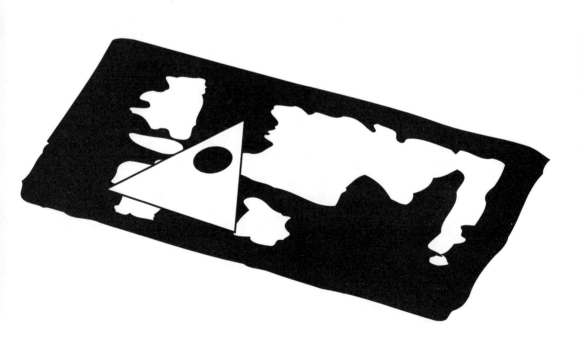

John Russo Writer/Director/Producer

1968 Night of the Living Dead
1981 Midnight
1996 Santa Claws
1998 Night of the Living Dead 30th Anniversary Edition

Movie Pain

Editor Paul McCollough and I were editing my movie MIDNIGHT on a Moviola machine in the headquarters of Hinzman Productions, which at the time was housed in a downtown Pittsburgh office building where almost all the other tenants were doctors and dentists. We were working on scene where a young man gets badly beaten by some thugs, so in trying to determine where to make our cut we had to listen to his loud screams over and over again.

Then the doorbell rang, and a very scared looking young man dressed in a suit and tie looked at me, and I looked at him, waiting for him to say something. Finally, his eyes wide with fear, he said, "Please... I hope you are not the dentist." I guess if I was making my "patients" scream like that, he did not want me operating on his teeth.

If you don't understand Latin. Don't read it out loud.

If you cut your finger don't bleed on a grave site OR over an ancient book of any kind.

Remember: Sex, Drinking, Drugs and Blood Rituals, don't mix.

Zombies
are stupid,
probably
the easiest
monster
to fool.
It's a
wonder more
folks don't try.
If
you find yourself
being chased
by a pack
of zombies,
try this:
Pretend you're
one of them.
Shuffle along,
grunt,
feign eating flesh.
How difficult
can it be ?
Blend in
until you can
escape.

If your friend is lost,
believe me;
they're lost.

If your dog is missing....
TOUGH !

If one of your friends tells you
"It's too late for me"
They're right.
Shoot Em.

If your friend wants to
remove a fly from your forehead
with a hatchet. See above.

Everyone
else is dead.
It's just you
and the monster.
Potentially this
is an advantage.
Stalemates
lead to sequels.
In B-Movies
sequels are the
ultimate form of
survival.

Don't stand outside a cabin and watch your friends fool around.

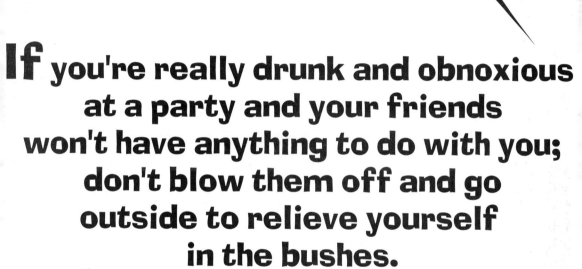

If you're really drunk and obnoxious at a party and your friends won't have anything to do with you; don't blow them off and go outside to relieve yourself in the bushes.

Never Say I'm not afraid of: Him , It or Them.

It's easy to avoid being killed by Godzilla.

He's huge, not particularly bright,

extremely clumsy, always snorting.

You can see him coming from a mile off.

The toughest thing might be Tokyo traffic.

Think bicycle !

Have you ever seen the big guy

waste a bicyclist ?

PEDAL POWER !

Where you are in a horror movie - timewise -

is critical. If the monster is chasing you

towards the beginning of the film,

it's okay to hide. It may even help you

survive by offering the audience a first

glimpse of the creature from your vantage.

On the other hand in the last five minutes

of any horror movie- and I mean any:

NO HIDING...... **RUN !**

Don't feel obligated to
check out every little
noise you hear at night !
The less curiosity
(and sexuality)
you exhibit, the more likely
you'll be around
for the sunrise.

At the first sign
of bad weather
CANCEL !
all your hiking/camping/
swimming/outdoor plans.
Thunderstorms arouse
even the most dormant
killer.

Be A Clown !
comic relief always
has a decent
chance of survival.

Don't
become a
night
security guard.

Never
be a
councilor
at a
summer camp.

Don't make fun of the nerdy or ugly kids in your school. Make them your friend.

If an old woman tells you not to: Go Somewhere, Do Something, or Meddle in Something. LISTEN !

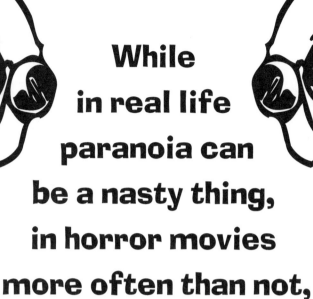

While
in real life
paranoia can
be a nasty thing,
in horror movies
more often than not,
it's the key to survival.
Chances are awfully good that
They Are Everywhere,
that the
**Walls Do Have
Ears and Eyes,**
and that
**Nefarious Forces Can
Read Your Every Thought.**
Don't let anyone fool you
into believing otherwise.

Don't
even think about
hitting a demon
over the head
with a shovel.

To him it's like
drinking
a cup of coffee,
it will simply
wake him up
and make him

very,

very

angry.

Don't Scream.[©]

-Surest way to die-
Run, throw things,
sweat like a pig
(by the way pigs don't sweat)
but Don't Scream[©]!
Hold your breath, let your eyes
go wide. Shhhhhh.
Simple matter of discipline

Gunnar Hansen

1974 Texas Chainsaw Massacre
1976 Demon Lover
1988 Hollywood Chainsaw Hookers
1991 Campfire Tales
1995 Mosquito
1995 Freakshow
1995 Exploding Angel
1997 Hellblock 13

How Not To Get A Date

Soon after Texas Chainsaw Massacre came out, a friend decided that I should use being a "Movie Star" to my advantage. One night he introduced me to one of the most beautiful women I had ever met. I caught my breath and had a hard time speaking. When she heard that not only was I an actor, but I had been in 'that' film, she snuggled up to me, stroking me with her voice. I mutely agreed to take her to see the movie the next night.

When I arrived she was almost panting... and so was I. She said we should come back to her apartment after the show and settle in on the couch. I could see where this was leading, and I could see I was going to like being a "Movie Star". She rubbed against me as we drove off to experience the "Texas Chainsaw Massacre".

Close together in the darkness of the theater, we watched me on the screen. We watched as I killed my first victim with a hammer. We watched my favorite scene, in which I impaled a girl on a meat hook. We watched the whole nasty, little story unwind.

She was strangely quiet on the way home. I did not mind. I was occupied with thoughts of was was to come next. As we walked to her door she fished her keys from her purse. She slid the keys into the lock. Thank you she said. "It was very interesting."

She opened the the door slightly and turned toward me. She then slipped through the door and slammed it shut. Evidently she had a bad feeling about the movie. And, as many others would in later years, she had confused me with Leatherface. So now when I meet a woman who wants to see the movie, I tell her I cant stand horror movies, they scare me, it usually works.

http://home.acadia.net/userpages/dog

Never

tune your radio to a top 40 station.
Serial killers love to target
people who listen to
rock n' roll, especially heavy metal.

If

you hear any sort of music
and you don't have a radio
leave the premises pronto.
Spontaneous music is always
accompanied by
MURDER !

Assume that your car will always start
(no matter how many mechanical problems it has)
UNLESS you are being chased by a monster of
genetic creation. Then, regardless, the engine
WILL NOT TURN OVER.
Simply get out of the car and run !
PS you will not have time to ring up AAA,
don't waste the cell phone call.

If you have
succeeded in starting your car,
you should still get out and flee on foot !
It doesn't matter how fast you drive,
the sick psycho will simply saunter
and catch-up to you.
Even if you're driving a Porche !

**Police never call for back-up.
They will typically:**

- **Not believe the panicked caller**

- **Underestimate the grizzly ghoul**

- **Approach the situation without sufficient precaution**

The end result?

**A totaled police vehicle
and severely dismembered flatfoot.**

The lesson ?

**Don't bother calling the cops for help,
even if your best friend is the
local sheriff's offspring**

Selected To Serve

HOOTERVILLE

POLICE

If you're in something
that ends with 'Part 2',
and realize you weren't in 'Part 1'
you most likely
won't make it to 'Part 3'.
SORRY.

If your flashlight batteries die........
SEE YA !

Remember:
Halloween night lasts
2 or 3 days.

Observe

photographs of Peter Lorre.
Note the beady eyes.
While in real life
a pair of beady eyes means nothing,
in B-Movies they always but always
denote evil. So if you meet a person
with beady eyes in a B-Movie be
very, very careful.

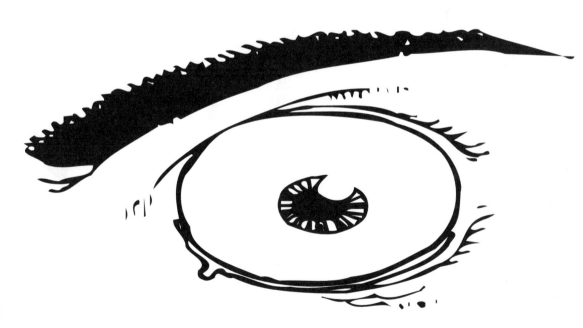

One of the worst things you can do is to torture or kill a defenseless baby monster. Sure, it might be tempting; often they're ugly buggers. Do yourself a favor,

Resist The Urge.

Debbie Rochon Actor/Writer

1994 Abducted II the Reunion
1995 Broadcast Bombshells
1997 Hellblock 13
1998 Terror Firmer
1998 Night of the Living Dead 30th Anniversary Edition
1999 In the Hood

Need A Hand ?

You could say I needed a hand while shooting my death scene from "Stumped". In this flick the villain is a severed hand that seeks to vindicate its owner's past. When I was to shoot the scene in which the hand strangles me to death, all I had to act with was a cheap plastic dime-store hand. Not only was it a challange to hold the limb in a position so that it looked real, but I also had to shake it in just the right way so it looked alive, not to mention act out my death scene with conviction. The hardest part was performing in a room filled with cast and crew busting-a-gut with laughter. Finally I had to become the ultimate B-movie Diva and demand a "closed set" while I shot the "hand job" scene (that's what the crew kindly christened it).

www.b-movie.com/debbie.html

Ron Bonk Director/Producer/Writer

1993 City of the Vampire
1997 Vicious Sweet
1998 Strawberry Estates
1999 Stumped

AAA Vampires ?

It was nighttime, raining, and the location was a dark alley. Before shooting, I had called the police and let them know about our shoot. I was using my truck to power one external lightduring the scene, but the battery had gotten damp and the car stalled out and refused to restart. I left my actors at the site and went to call AAA. When I came back, a spotlight suddenly hit me in the face and before I could thank all the little people I saw the police had surrounded my truck, guns drawn ! It seems no one had let them know about our shoot and they thought they had happened upon a drug deal ! And one with vampires to boot ! Luckily, I convinced them everything was cool. They finally left, with one officer yelling back " you better be careful next time or someone might get their head blown off."

As A General Rule:
Don't
Do Anything That Opens A Portal
To Hell !

If A Character

From A Video Game

Starts Talking To You On The Screen:
Throw The Game Away !

Try Checkers.

WEAPONRY TIPS

If you're working with a chainsaw
remember this:
ghouls can function very well
without limbs !
Cutting pieces off will only
create more mutants.
What you want to do is separate the
head from the body
and remove the heart.
If it's still coming after you,
turn the chainsaw on yourself !

Don't let the monster have the

last laugh !

Always
grab a loaded gun.
Throwing an unloaded gun at a Zombie
will only piss it off.

If
you get the opportunity to actually

stab the monster with a knife.
DON'T
leave the knife in his chest

and walk away !
Always
take your cutlery with you !

When in doubt
SHOOT !

this applies to the following:

- **People you don't recognize**

- **People with farm implements**

- **Oversized animals**

- **Friends ?**

- **Things surrounded by fog**

- **Clowns**

- **Mimes (They are probably OK, but shoot them anyway)**

Blowtorches
**are the ideal weapon of choice.
Not too expensive,
don't need a license to own one,
yet infinitely potent
for dispatching various fiends.**

**Remember:
All
Asian people
are
Black Belts
in Karate.**

If

a killer

or monster

is in your house

should you....

a) **As quietly as possible slip out the nearest door and run far away...**

OR

b) **Run screaming through your house and lock yourself in a bathroom with no windows.**

Don't think too hard.

If
your chainsaw
or
machete is missing...
That's not all that's
going to be
missing !

If
you've
reached the point
that you need to check
if someone is buried
in their grave...
You might as well
dig yours.

SCIENCE
PROBLEMS

Fred Olen Ray   Producer/Director

1983 Biohazard
1987 Hollywood Chainsaw Hookers
1990 Evil Toons
1993 Dinosaur Island

Bite Me ?

While on location in India, filming the final conflict for "Operation Cobra", a Roger Corman martial arts epic, our hero, Don "The Dragon" Wilson was to kick the bad guy backwards into an aquarium housing a live cobra. After a few camera-cuts the bad guy was supposed to stiffen up and reach behind his neck and bring out this snake (which had supposedly bitten him) and then slump over and play dead.

The snake, we were assured had no poison left in him and if handled gently had no desire to bite . (At one point the snake escaped. I recaptured him myself- with photo to prove it, and was not bitten.) Cameras went rolling, the actor reached behind his neck. A hidden Indian kid handed him the snake and he started to bring the creature around front. As he did I noticed the snake sink his teeth into the actors ring finger and dig in; I mean it really was not going to let go !

I leaned over to my camera man, Gary Grauer and whispered into his ear - "Is that thing biting him ?" Gary said, "Yeah, what should we do ?" I said " Do not stop shooting !"

Anthony Tipone   Writer/Editor

14 year editor of Fangoria (The world's best-selling horror magazine)
Men Makeup and Monsters; Hollywood Masters of Illusion and FX (St. Martin's Press)

Snuff Said

During my 14 year tenure at the Fangoria helm, I have met the full spectrum of horror and exploitation personalities, from the big to the small. But as a writer and editor, I usually find the the best stories, anecdotes and controversies coming from the people who work down and dirty in the trenches of low-budget movies.

One of my all-time favorite Fangoria interviews was with one of the all-time worst filmmakers, Roberta Findlay, who contributed to such memorable gems as "Shiek of the Mutilated", The "Oracle" and the notorious "Snuff", which she shot. Findlay was full of hilarious stories of vomiting Argentinean bus drivers, crazy feminists who stalked her, anti-Semite investors. Then she told me of the fate of her husband, Michael Findlay, who had directed "Snuff", the controversial 1976 film that allegedly featured real human slaughter. "He was the guy who was decapitated on the top of the old Pan Am building when the helecopter tipped over, "she told me nonchalantly. Grasping for something to politely console her, I said, "Gee, I am sorry. What a tragedy." "Oh that is OK," she responded, "We were divorced."

If A Meteor Strikes
Near You Remember....
It's Not A Souvenir

Strange Lights
That Emenate
From Rooms Or Fields...
ARE BAD !

If
You Hear
Weird Music
Run !

Nine out of ten aliens are evil.

Since there are no laws against offing creatures from another planet, shoot first ask questions later. Remember aliens have no rights. They're not human, they're not even mammals. The law can't touch you ... Only PETA.

Don't
Volunteer to be a medical or psychological test subject

Never trust a robot !

If you find yourself sucked into another dimension, go with the flow. Keep calm. Once you have arrived in the alternate realm, don't be shy, ask questions of the inhabitants; they know where the portal is.

You

can tell you're

hallucinating

in a horror movie

if all the things

you're seeing

have blurry edges.

Mad Scientists have the best sense of humor, second only to the Devil.

Even a very intelligent group of scientists will split up to look for the alien.

Believe me,
Danger lies within slime.
You will die a horrible death,
or be taken over if
you're frozen with fear.
Slime is slow ; move, and
trust me,
don't pick it up !

Lloyd Kaufman

President Troma Entertainment

1985 Toxic Avenger   **1986 Class of Nuke 'Em High**
1989 Toxic Avenger, Part 2   **1989 Toxic Avenger, Part 3**
1990 Sgt. Kabukiman N.Y.P.D.   **1995 Tromeo and Juliet**
1998 Terror Firmer

You Call That A Fire

On a Troma film I recently directed, we had a major problem with the stuntmen. We paid an exorbitant sum (in excess of $ 39.99) to two people to perform and/or coordinate the stunts, but received nothing but a hard lesson in return. This stuntman was engaged contractually to perform a very specific number and kind of stunts, in which they were to prove their competency by providing a videotape of themselves performing the feat previously.

Every stunt was f***ed up. When the stunt was supposed to be "full body burn", as called for in his contract, the guy's upper back was sprinkled with tiny tongues of flame as he screamed like a nancy boy for someone to put him out. We put up with this for a while but one of our dedicated production assistants would have gladly covered themselves in gasoline and lit a match for free.

On the day he was to do a high fall at a site which he had long before reconnoitered and approved, Stunt Boy changed the location of the jump. It seemed the jump was too high for the three cardboard boxes and wet sponge he had brought to break his fall. He had promised me personally to bring a giant airbag to break a huge high fall. The resulting jump was comparable in danger and excitement to watching an elderly woman step off a public bus.

I should have fired those a**holes the first day of preproduction when they would not leave my office without being paid in advance for a job they had not even begun. They had never provided the tape and,predictably, everything they touched turned to muddy black s**t. I knew they were going to suck but I "wussed out" (because I am a "wuss" and that is what "wusses" do). Here comes the lesson learned: F**k being an equal opportunity employer-- be an equal opportunity firer ! Whatever their skin color, religious orientation, sexual preference, body shape; if you get a bad feeling about someone, fire em ! If you dont, do not bitch about the concequences.

On a lighter note, we all felt better about the stunts when one of our production assistants smashed and overturned a van while running a red light in Brooklyn. Although he was unhurt, he did manage to spill hundreds of thousands of dollars worth of equiptment all over the street. Typically.. there was no camera there to capure this excitement and the accident was not covered by our insurance

If A Package
Is Accidentally
Delivered To You From A
Museum
Or
Scientific Sounding Place...

Burn It !

LOCATION LOCATION LOCATION

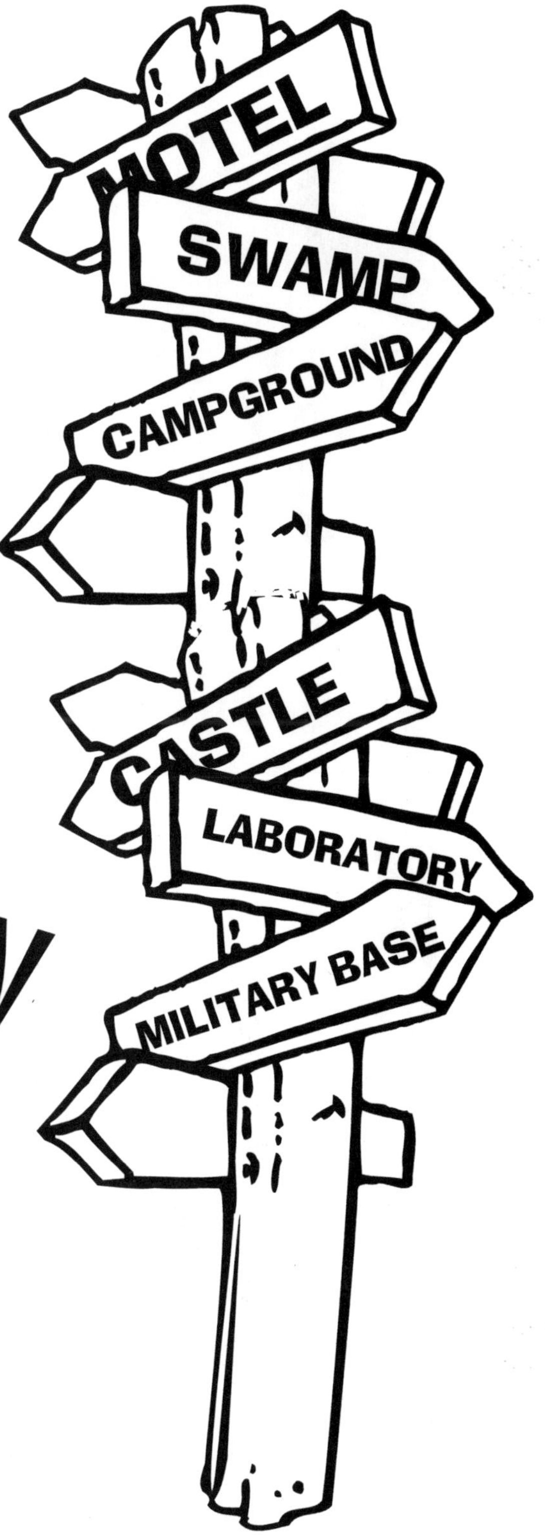

MOTEL

SWAMP

CAMPGROUND

CASTLE

LABORATORY

MILITARY BASE

Don't
leave the interstate:
EVER !

ROUTE
666

Never
pick up
a hitchhiker
on a
deserted road;
especially in :
Wisconsin,
Texas
or the Ozarks

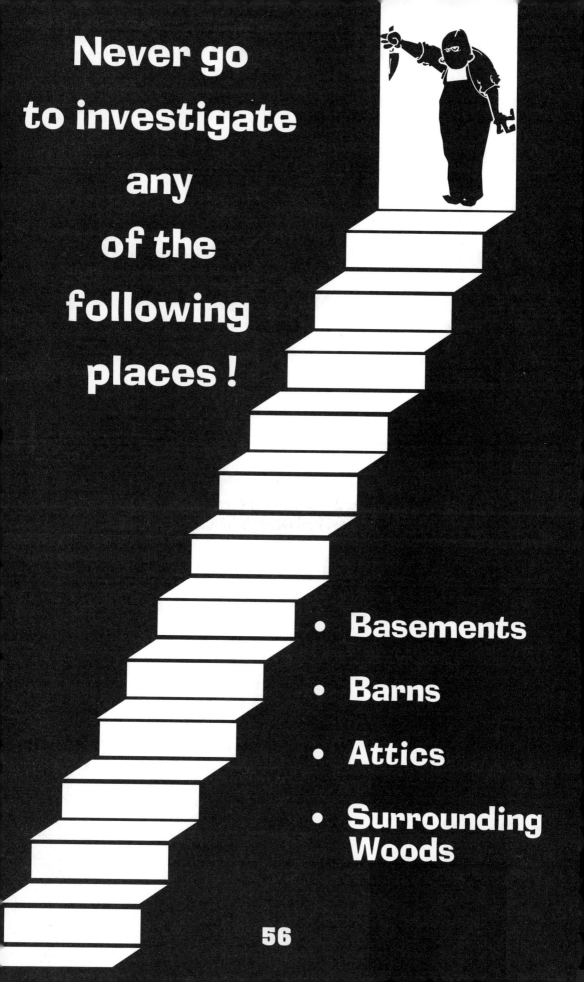

Never go
to investigate
any
of the
following
places !

- **Basements**

- **Barns**

- **Attics**

- **Surrounding
  Woods**

**Real estate market being what it is;
if you inherit a spooky-looking
Gothic castle in Europe from some
distant relative - SELL IT !
Make a tidy profit, avoid being
terrorized, mutilated or killed.
Have Fun, Spend The Money !**

**Abandoned military bases,
mansions,
hotels and villages
were abandoned for a reason.**

Carel Struycken Actor

1978 Sgt. Peppers Lonely Hearts Club Band
1980 Die Laughing
1987 Witches Of Eastwick
1991 Addams Family
1993 Addams Family Values
1994 Oblivion
1997 Men In Black

Could I Have Some More Please ?

It was really hard making the Oblivion films for Full Moon. Everyone complained and I was in the middle range of complainers. The girls I think were the hardcore complainers. Romania, where we shot the film, is a beautiful country, but its infrastructure was completely demolished by one of its past dictators. I am a vegetarian and the only thing I could eat there was Goulash ! We had very long shooting days and I would have to organize a trip to the market so I could buy some vegetables, then bribe the cook to let me use the pots because they refused to cook any vegetables. It was an ordeal just to feed myself. Then an Italian film crew came to town and they chartered a truck to drive from Italy with cooked meals for them ! Once they came to town I got a good lunch. Every night people on our film were really starving ! When a soccer teem moved into our hotel, they brought their own food, so we would stand near their dining room like hungry urchins begging for food. Even someone like Julie Newmar who is this stately lady who can stop any room she walks into, at a certain point grabbed a little bowl of left over Parmesean cheese and attacked it ! We all stood at the bowl like a bunch of thieves !

Mike Mayo Author

VideoHound's Video Premieres (Visible Ink Press)
VideoHound's Horror Show   (Visible Ink Press))

Say What ?

For a reviewer, most of the really funny moments in B-movies come from dialogue, sometimes they are meant to be humorous. For example, there is a moment in "Tromeo and Juliet" when Juliet says, "Parting is such sweet sorrow" and Tromeo answers, "Yeah, it sucks." More often though they are unintentional, like the funeral scene in the Bo Derek/Anthony Quinn epic "Ghosts Can't Do It " where the preacher asks the retorical question, "What is life ?" and then answers himself with, "It is the breath of the buffalo in the wintertime. Yes, it is a reminder to us all that we take time to smell the buffalo breath."

FEMALE TROUBLE

Ladies, have fun now but remember 3 simple words:

SLUTS DON'T SURVIVE

If you are a female and not a real blond, don't fake it, **IT WILL KNOW.**

Don't invite all your girlfriends over to your house for a fun little seance... Try checkers and popcorn.

Lesbian vampires
are delightful
to look at...

**from
a distance.**

No matter what time of day
you decide to head out
and kill the vampire
once you walk outside
it's 5 minutes before sundown

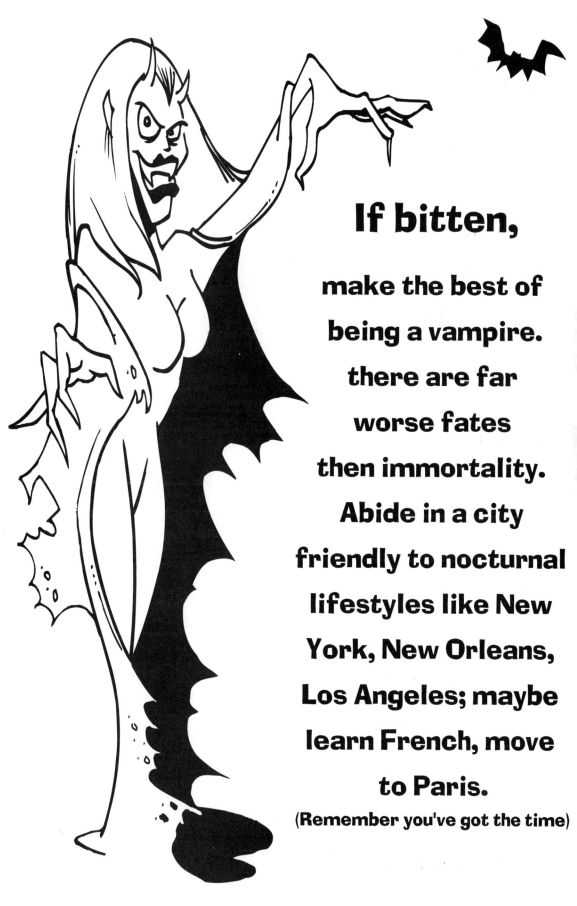

If bitten,

make the best of
being a vampire.
there are far
worse fates
then immortality.
Abide in a city
friendly to nocturnal
lifestyles like New
York, New Orleans,
Los Angeles; maybe
learn French, move
to Paris.
(Remember you've got the time)

Never buy old books mirrors or wooden boxes from an antique store.

If you're a female and you're sent to clean up an old abandoned house or office

Remember:
Lingerie is not the wardrobe of choice for cleaning professionals.

If

you're a woman

caught in a

contemporary horror movie,

toughness is everything.

Feminine wiles won't work

with today's monster

(King Kong and Fay Wray

was long ago) Be a broad;

if necessary, a bitch.

Study Sigorney Weaver

in the

"Aliens" movies.

Zachary W. Snygg Actor/Writer/Director

1992 Kudos from Pseudo Intellectuals (Films Around the World)
1996 Blood Bullets Buffoons (E.I. Independent Cinema)
1999 In The Hood (E.I. Independent Cinema)

Less Is Not Always More

Producing independent feature films is often a nightmare of grand proportions. Most "Hollywood" films (as some would deem "real movies") include a cast and crew of thousands. Most of my films include a cast and crew of two- me and my timid brother Spencer. About four years ago when my brother and I were shooting "Blood Bullets Buffoons", I had wished that I had had a cast and crew of at least five. Spencer and I were shooting late at night in which a "clown" (reluctantly portrayed by Spencer) drives a car decorated with animal balloons and picks up a deranged hitchhiker (brilliantly portrayed by myself ! ok. Adequately portrayed by myself).

The shooting day started out to be more fun than humanly possible. Spencer and I blew up (by mouth because we broke our air pump) 130 balloons, and we twisted them into animals. None of these even remotely resembled animals- more like amoebas. Once the balloons were completed, we went outside and proceeded to decorate our $ 700.00 car with them. About half of them popped or floated away.

Once shooting began it started to rain heavily. I personally love rain, but I do not like filming in it. More importantly, I enjoyed it much less when the ground is laid with exposed 120 volt electrical cords powering our lights and camera. Spencer and I traded off "camera man"duties while each one filmed the other acting. This made life even more exciting because everytime the "camera man" turned the camera on, we were blasted with eneough electricity to make Don King envious.

In the final shot of the clown/hitchhiker scene, Spencer and I appear together. I had to start the camera and then run into the shot with my brother picking me up in the clown car. This was a good idea, but, unfortunately, my brother proceeded to drive me around the block. I told him that I needed to go back and stop the camera. Buy the time I got back to the camera, we had run out of film. I had no film left and the shoot was over. Film costs about $ 130.00 a roll.

What had we learned from this ? Well five people would have been much better than two. Two actors, a camera man a sound guy and another person to tell me not to shoot in the rain because the shots would n ot match. You know it is raining hard here and not at all there and so hard you can not see the guy over there. This is why Hollywood made "rain" machines.

If you're a female understand that your clothing will automatically become tear-away once the bad guy enters the scene.

Girls remember:

Haunted houses

are never locked,

but you can be sure

that once you need

a place to hide,

every other building

in the world

will be locked.

Hygiene
is not
important:

under no

circumstances

bathe

and certainly

Never

take a shower.

Honorary Tip

"If someone asks you if you're a god......
SAY YES ! "

(Ernie Hudson: Ghost Busters)

The List

Everybody loves lists
This will be your post graduate course
in B-movie survival...
How many have you seen ?

(List is Chronological)

- [ ] **FREAKS   1932**
- [ ] **THE RAVEN 1935**
- [ ] **THE TERROR OF TINY TOWN 1938**
- [ ] **RETURN OF DR. X 1939** (HUMPHREY BOGART'S ONLY HORROR MOVIE)
- [ ] **ZOMBIES ON BROADWAY 1945**
- [ ] **DEVIL GIRL FROM MARS 1954**
- [ ] **A BUCKET OF BLOOD 1959**
- [ ] **THE HOUSE ON HAUNTED HILL 1959**
- [ ] **THE LITTLE SHOP OF HORRORS 1960**
- [ ] **PEEPING TOM 1960**
- [ ] **PSYCHO 1960**
- [ ] **CARNIVAL OF SOULS 1962**
- [ ] **WHAT EVER HAPPENED TO BABY JANE ? 1962**
- [ ] **THE HAUNTING 1963**
- [ ] **COLOR ME BLOOD RED 1964**
- [ ] **2000 MANIACS 1964**
- [ ] **FASTER PUSSYCAT KILL! KILL! 1965**
- [ ] **NIGHT OF THE LIVING DEAD 1968**
- [ ] **THE DUNWICH HORROR 1969**
- [ ] **BLOOD & LACE 1970**
- [ ] **LUST FOR A VAMPIRE 1970**
- [ ] **THE VAMPIRE LOVERS 1970**
- [ ] **THE HITCHHIKER 1971**
- [ ] **THE DEVILS 1971**
- [ ] **WILLARD 1971**
- [ ] **BLACKULA 1972**
- [ ] **LAST HOUSE ON THE LEFT 1972**
- [ ] **THE RATS ARE COMING ! THE WEREWOLVES ARE HERE 1972**
- [ ] **BLACKENSTEIN 1973**
- [ ] **THE CARS THAT EAT PEOPLE 1973**
- [ ] **THE EXORCIST 1973**
- [ ] **SILENT NIGHT BLOODY NIGHT 1973**
- [ ] **BARN OF THE NAKED DEAD 1973**

- [ ] **FOXY BROWN** 1974
- [ ] **THE TEXAS CHAINSAW MASSACRE** 1974
- [ ] **CARRIE** 1976
- [ ] **ERASERHEAD** 1976
- [ ] **THE OMEN** 1976
- [ ] **CYCLE VIXENS** 1977
- [ ] **THE HILLS HAVE EYES** 1977
- [ ] **HALLOWEEN** 1978
- [ ] **THE AMITYVILLE HORROR** 1979
- [ ] **THE DRILLER KILLER** 1979
- [ ] **PHANTASM** 1979
- [ ] **WHEN A STRANGER CALLS** 1979
- [ ] **CARNY** 1980
- [ ] **FRIDAY THE 13TH** 1980
- [ ] **THE HOWLING** 1980
- [ ] **MOTHERS DAY** 1980
- [ ] **MS 45** 1980
- [ ] **PROM NIGHT** 1980
- [ ] **MOTEL HELL** 1980
- [ ] **THE SHINING** 1980
- [ ] **BASKET CASE** 1981
- [ ] **GHOST STORY** 1981
- [ ] **THE HAND** 1981
- [ ] **MIDNIGHT** 1981
- [ ] **CREEPSHOW** 1982
- [ ] **THE EVIL DEAD** 1982
- [ ] **POLTERGEIST** 1982
- [ ] **SLUMBER PARTY MASSACRE** 1982
- [ ] **ZOMBIE ISLAND MASSACRE** 1982
- [ ] **DEATHSTALKER** 1983
- [ ] **THE HUNGER** 1983
- [ ] **SLEEPAWAY CAMP** 1983
- [ ] **TICKS** 1983
- [ ] **CUJO** 1983
- [ ] **BLOODSUCKERS FROM OUTER SPACE** 1984
- [ ] **THE SEVEN MAGNIFICENT GLADIATOR** 1984
- [ ] **SILENT NIGHT DEADLY NIGHT** 1984
- [ ] **TERMINATOR** 1984
- [ ] **FRIGHT NIGHT** 1985
- [ ] **RE-ANIMATOR** 1985

- [ ] **RETURN OF THE LIVING DEAD 1985**
- [ ] **THE TOXIC AVENGER 1985**
- [ ] **APRIL FOOLS DAY 1986**
- [ ] **BLUE VELVET 1986**
- [ ] **CHOPPING MALL 1986**
- [ ] **THE HITCHER 1986**
- [ ] **REFORM SCHOOL GIRLS 1986**
- [ ] **STRIPPED TO KILL 1986**
- [ ] **WITCHBOARD 1986**
- [ ] **BLOOD DINER 1987**
- [ ] **BRAIN DAMAGE 1987**
- [ ] **CANNIBAL HOOKERS 1987**
- [ ] **EVIL DEAD II 1987**
- [ ] **HELLRAISER 1987**
- [ ] **HENRY..PORTRAIT OF A SERIAL KILLER 1987**
- [ ] **KILLER KLOWNS FROM OUTER SPACE 1987**
- [ ] **THE LOST BOYS 1987**
- [ ] **NEAR DARK 1987**
- [ ] **SORORITY BABES IN THE SLIMEBALL BOWL-A-RAMA 1987**
- [ ] **ANGEL HEART 1987**
- [ ] **HARD TICKET TO HAWAII 1987**
- [ ] **PUMPKINHEAD 1987**
- [ ] **CHILD'S PLAY 1988**
- [ ] **ELVIRA, MISTRESS OF THE DARK 1988**
- [ ] **THE WEREWOLF VS. THE VAMPIRE WOMEN** (BLOOD MOON) **1989**
- [ ] **THEY LIVE 1988**
- [ ] **PET CEMETARY 1989**
- [ ] **PUPPET MASTER 1989**
- [ ] **EVIL TOONS 1990**
- [ ] **FRANKENHOOKER 1990**
- [ ] **ADDAMS FAMILY 1991**
- [ ] **BODY PARTS 1991**
- [ ] **PEOPLE UNDER THE STAIRS 1991**
- [ ] **THE SILENCE OF THE LAMBS 1991**
- [ ] **SUBSPECIES 1991**
- [ ] **LEPRECHAUN 1992**
- [ ] **THE CROW 1993**
- [ ] **CEMETARY MAN 1995**
- [ ] **SCREAM 1996**